Flying with Chains

Flying with Chains

KAPIL RAJ

Anecdote
Publishing House

Anecdote
Publishing House

Anecdote Publishing House
E-35-A, E Block, Gali No. 2, Ganesh Nagar,
Pandav Nagar Complex, Delhi - 110092

Published by Anecdote Publishing House

First Edition 2023

ISBN: 9788195890750

MRP: ₹ 149.00

Book Promoted and Marketed by Champ Readers Pvt. Ltd.

Layout and Cover by Anecdote
Printed in India

*To all the free souls,
hurt, chained, and caged
by social rules and
fabrications*

Change Stories by

Kapil Raj

Change Stories by Kapil Raj is an amalgamation of five independent short stories: ***Kuroopa, A Gutterful Life, First Love Many Times, Flying with Chains, and A Mother By The Window.***

Advancement of humankind invariably poses new challenges to the existing social order in society. It weakens the bondages enforced by patriarchal rules, paving the way for societal awakening. However, every ounce of progress leaves behind some debris in its wake. Failure to recognise this debris or 'problem' can bestow acute misery and suffering in the lives of people. Going back and snipping the problem in the bud is usually more cumbersome than revolting and moving forward.

If only there was an easy way out.

True social development cannot be achieved without breaking existing stereotypes and adapting our mindsets to the subsequent changes.

Each short story interweaves a heartening story with a deeply imbibed social issue, hardened public belief, and associated fabrications. As you read the narrative, you watch and evolve with the characters, sometimes feeling yourself in them – empathising in circumstances that may or may not have existed in your lives. The stories will highlight the suffering that was never supposed to take place had we brought about a meaningful change for ourselves and others in the society.

However, there's always a first, and it can start here.

We live how we think, and we think how we choose to live.
Progress is hard; change is heroic.

Acknowledgements

Every beginning has a story. We often emphasise too much on the journey and the end goal, forgetting all about that *first step*.

When I commenced writing *ENDURER A Rape Story*, I was scared spending nights on the outcome. From the inception of the idea to getting the story published, three years passed. The book finally, reached the hands of readers and found love in a way I had never imagined.

For the first time, when I held the mic in a room full of young students to speak on the subject (rape and sexual assaults) which is considered one of the biggest taboo in the Indian households, my hands trembled, yet I took that leap.

By the end of each of session, I was gifted emotions, witnessed appreciation and respect. It was a dream come true. But a thought lingered behind. What next? What topic should I pick? Will I be able to justify the appreciation and recognition I received? The turmoil was too much. For a moment, I felt giving up. In those times, there are people who stand with you, influencing in ways which do not let yourself stop and take on unfamiliar paths.

They are my parents, my wife Payal, my sister Dimple and my son Hetarth. I owe you.

Pulkit, Thank You. You always stood along. When I simply could not progress further, your faith in me made me hold on and continue to move.

Tatiana, I am grateful for your persuasion and astute conversations. You incepted ideas on which I was able to write and build these stories.

Tina, you have my gratitude. You chiselled out the entire work with your editing and added a clear voice to the words.

Sincere thanks to Anecdote Publishers & Sagar Azad, who trusted me with my unconventional project and extended all support to get published.

And most importantly, I would like to thank all my readers. Your reviews, personal texts, praises and critiques motivated me to walk through this journey.

1

Taruni paused her iPod and climbed down from the upper berth of the train coach. She waved her hand at the passenger who was occupying her seat, indicating that she wanted him to move – he was probably ticketless and riding for free. The contemptuous jerk of her hand seemed to enrage the gentleman, and he eyed her scornfully – it was almost as if she had disturbed him in the middle of something important. However, he knew he was in the wrong and obliged to follow. She looked under the seat for her shoes and found them tucked beside the other passenger's suitcase. After taking a sip of water, she unceremoniously dumped a half-read magazine, an unfinished packet of chips, and a sealed bottle of coke into her open backpack.

The train slowed down, and the announcements began. She stood in the line of passengers, aiming towards the exit. The multitude of unpleasant smells inside the coach disrupted her constant worry. The train stopped with a jolt. It was time to disembark. She shouldered her backpack and pulled her heavy, wheeled suitcase behind her. As she stepped down from the train, trying to balance her luggage between the platform and train's edge, a familiar arm intervened and effortlessly picked her suitcase. It was Kunal, beaming with his signature gummy smile.

"How is dad?" Taruni asked impatiently.

"Better. He is resting now." Kunal replied, leading the way out.

Taruni barely knew the departing passengers but felt she could relate to them somehow. Succumbing to the dressing etiquette and fashion styles that bigger cities embody; experiencing homesickness, nostalgia, and anticipation about things that will never be the same; the guilt of changing one's personality, fear of the future, and feeling stressed because of excessive hardships – your home becoming nothing but a casual weekend getaway.

As they hustled towards the car, her eyes flickered over the empty stairs of a distant overbridge. Her breath paused, and a barrage of memories flashed across her mind. She was winded for a moment, but kept moving. This experience was the first. It would repeat every time she returned to this place in the future. Wounds do not heal; we just learn to live with them.

Parents, brothers, sisters, and family members waited outside the station, anticipating happiness. They pushed their way through the hawkers.

Taruni sat in the car, completely dazed, and Kunal drove off. She did not look at him even once except to gaze down at his loose jeans and flashy shirt.

"How is college?" asked Kunal.

"Good."

"Do you remember Baluni uncle?"

"Of course I do. I have only been away for a few months. It's not like I am returning after a decade," said Taruni, still not meeting his eyes.

"He was getting that school building constructed."

"Ya, he fell from the terrace of that very building."

Taruni's eyes widened, and she finally looked at Kunal. Baluni uncle lived in their colony and was like a living curse to the children. His bungalow was next to the society garden, and he would repeatedly yell at the playful, noise-making children all the time. Everyone disliked him. He kicked stray dogs and threw hot water on any passing animals like cows or monkeys. Only God understood his concepts about life. Then one day, when people heard he was opening a school, they couldn't believe their ears. Baluni was anything but an educator. He was a joke. What kind of education would students receive at his school? For Mr Baluni, it was all about the money.

"How?" Taruni enquired out of curiosity.

"Well, the construction was complete. They were doing some photography for the local newspaper and Baluni uncle wanted himself silhouetted against the sun. The terrace was on the highest floor of the building. The photographers warned that it wasn't the best idea, but you know how he was. His shoe got stuck in his pants and he fell, breaking almost every bone in his body."

There was a moment of silence. Taruni knew Kunal was trying not to chuckle.

"Stop it!" she said, refraining herself from laughing. "You are making me laugh."

"And… and, Sharma uncle got kidnapped."

"What?"

"Ya. They found him in Gorakhpur. And Anuj bhaiya..."

"Yes, what about him?"

"His wife left him over a fight in the middle of a society function."

Taruni was dumbfounded. She remembered how her flatmates and college fellows talked about giving space and minding their own business. But things were the exact opposite here. She had come home to meet her father, who recently suffered a heart attack, but was bombarded with all the society gossip within a minute of reaching the city. The boundary of personal territory was trying to comprehend the influx of scandalous information. Here, personal space meant little. Here, everybody knew what the others were up to around them.

Kunal tapped on Taruni's head, jolting her out of her reverie.

"I have not left your father's side even for a minute. It is good you came, but you should not have interrupted your studies. Calm down; the worst is over."

Taruni watched Kunal. Even her mother said the same thing. 'What will you do?' 'He is sleeping,' etc. But it's not just love, but the guilt of not being around your family in times of need that pulls you towards them. Taruni sighed and eagerly waited to reach home.

2

Yatin, Taruni and Kunal had a shared childhood; they all grew up together. Not only were they classmates in school, they were also next-door neighbours and their homes were close enough to play throw and catch ball from their respective terraces. The society they lived in was adjacent to the railway station. The distance was significant by road, but was extremely less on foot. Cross a wall at the tail-end of the society, walk a bit, climb over the boundary wall of the railway station, and one would reach the spot our protagonists frequented – an overbridge on a railway track. The trio had no recollection of when they first found it. Their study sessions, gossip meetings, after school hangouts all transpired at the bridge. They would lounge on its stairs on the busiest of days, if only for a few minutes. It was a comfortable spot; air jettisoned by the passing of trains that would regularly strike the bridge, acting as natural air conditioner.

The entire station staff knew the kids since Taruni's father worked in railways and was deployed at the same station. The trio would sometimes get their hands on free samosas or leftover refreshments from the trains. Life could not have been better for them, but only at the peak does calamity strike; especially when you are expecting it the least.

"Where are you going?" asked mother.

Taruni gaped at her mother with confusion. Why

was she asking her questions about something pertaining to her daily routine?

"Taruni, sit here and try to understand," said mother. Taruni listened to her and sat on the sofa.

"My words might irritate you, but you are not a little girl anymore. You are hanging out with those boys all the time. People ..."

"Oh mom! They are Kunal and Yatin, for God's sake!" exclaimed Taruni with exasperation, jumping from her seat.

"As we become older, things change. We need to learn and adapt according to our surroundings. You hear me! Neighbours talk behind our backs all the time. Your friends are like family, so you can meet them here or at their homes. Why the secluded bridge? And what is the point of your daily meetings? You go to school together, attend the same tuition. What more is there to talk about?

Answer me."

"What has changed all of a sudden, mom? It has been our den since childhood, a place of solace. You think we go there to chit-chat, but imagine a lonely meeting with ourselves. There are days when we don't even talk."

"What do you mean by this?"

"Hah! You won't understand."

"I was also a teenager once, okay? And…"

Taruni pressed her palms to her ears to stop listening. Any conflict, big or small, would culminate in this sentence to conclude the discussion. She was tired of it.

She grabbed her bicycle and rode away. The

frequent lectures were getting on her nerves. She was a growing kid, trying to understand herself. She was learning to react to situations, gauge new feelings, and discover the world in her own way. And suddenly, one fine day, she was made the subject of observation and correction. Her future became a cause of concern for others. Out of nowhere, random individuals judged her for what she wore, who she hung out with, and when she returned home at night. Meeting her friends had become an issue for a random auntie who had no clue about her own life. And Taruni was required to abide by some stranger's unsaid, unwritten expectations. Why?

She parked her bicycle next to the bridge and walked up to the top. Kunal stood in a corner, watching the sunset, while Yatin was busy doodling in a notebook. A train had just left the station and she could see several people mulling about the exit. Everyone seemed to be in a rush. Taruni would always pause and observe the passengers. They had a purpose, however fleeting it was, and this knowledge gave her peace.

3

"Papa, I need money. That tuition class is a must for my entrance exams," requested Kunal, with a touch of impatience.

Mohan Lal glowered at his son while he counted a wad of notes with his saliva-smeared fingers. The manager of the showroom, a close family acquaintance, giggled.

"Son, what is the point of education? These days,

after spending a whole amount of money on engineering and MBA, children just leave their jobs to open businesses. Jeetu, what do you call them?"

"Antree-puner, sir."

"Yes, yes, that only. That son of Agrawal Ji, after draining lakhs of rupees, now sells burgers in a truck. So shameless. And he proudly calls it – Jeetu, what do you call it?"

"Star-pat," replied Jeetu.

Kunal thought if any sensible person heard these people speak of 'entrepreneur' and 'startup' this way, they would probably have a mild heart attack. "Yes, yes. What is all this? You are the prince of the city. This business, all these showrooms, are waiting for you to join. We can't wait for you to take this burden off our shoulders and conquer the market," said the manager, through tobacco-stained teeth.

"Sir, are you finally retiring?" said someone in the staff and everyone broke into laughter.

"Shut up! Go clean the window on the second floor. Careless people," Mohan Lal said grumpily.

"Papa!" shouted Kunal, requesting attention.

Mohan looked at his son with reproach. He had no idea whether to be happy or sad about him. Kunal was just supposed to understand basic mathematics in order to count notes. The rest was simply unnecessary. Mohan himself had studied only till the fifth grade and then left to try his hand in the real world. Now he was a millionaire, owner of numerous showrooms, hospitals, and malls. He was the chairman of the district-level business committee and all his son wanted to do was leave this empire, crack some exams, get a job, and then what? Work like a labourer under some metro travelling, EMI burdened manager? Mohan called them educated illiterates. Excessive education was for fools. On-hand experience was the only way to succeed.

"When are you joining the business?" asked Kunal's father. He still hoped to change his son's mind without resistance. He would have done it long ago if he had to do it by force.

"Papa, I am just a kid. Let me live my life. I'm asking for money to study, not for something frivolous that most boys my age are into," Kunal said, rolling his eyes and trying to explain how lucky his father was to have him.

"I will break your bones, your friends' bones, the bones of the owner of the place where you will try to spend on 'frivolity'. Understood?"

"Yes." That went really wrong. Kunal realised his mistake.

"So what tuition?"

"This is for my engineering exam, an extra course for IIT and –"

"Take this money and go buy some shoes. No extra tuition, ok? You are not leaving this city. After you finish high school, you are either joining the business right away or attending college while working with me. In this city!"

Kunal was a nerd who was deeply interested in physics and mathematics. He had a sharp mind and was always looking to unravel the mysteries of the world. There are two schools of thought when it comes to the creation of the Universe, one stemming from faith and the other from science. Some people think that God created everything, but for Kunal, the only way to understand this physical world was through the laws of physics. From the solar system to an atom, physics had the wherewithal to explain the stunning architecture of God. Kunal dreamt of being like Hawkins.

At home, he had only revealed his wish to clear IIT; his father would have never understood his true dream. All they wanted was to get tobacco-chewing people to pasture a way for him in life. He had topped in physics in the year-end exams and all his teachers had high expectations of him. His father was a different matter altogether.

Kunal did not touch the money and just stormed out. Mohan Lal's staff eyed the dough greedily and cursed Kunal in their minds. What an irony. Some can go to any lengths to lay their hands on these strips of paper, while others hold no value for it whatsoever. Whether money can buy everything or not, that's not the point. It is a person's heart that assigns value to it. For Mohan, the hand offering the notes meant everything. He had sacrificed the good years of his life to be where he was today, yet he couldn't convince his only son.

4

Kunal leaned on an iron pillar, viewing the distant trees, subconsciously estimating their impact on the coolness of the air. Taruni carelessly lounged on a stair, watching the opposite side of the platform. She could see a girl jumping around her dad. A young toddler was trying to follow them, and would occasionally fall, resulting in a burst of collective laughter. There were no definitions, no boundaries, no judgement to follow.

"You guys have been keeping low for days," said Yatin, munching on a samosa.

"I am sick and tired of these restrictions. It is too much," said Taruni with frustration.

"I will throw my phone away if I see one more Reel on motherly love or anything related to home being a paradise. I mean, fine, I love her, and she loves me, but do we understand each other? What good is love if we cannot respect each other's expectations and keep trying to restrain our loved ones?" she continued.

Kunal and Yatin eyed each other. They were taken aback at this sudden outburst. Taruni's voice was brimming with anger – way more than usual.

"Do our parents own us? Are we their property? No means no – they say. Murder our feelings for the things they couldn't do in their lives? They keep saying they are being protective. But by doing so, are they trying to make their children stronger or weaker? They are concealing us from the hardships of life. How is that a good thing?"

Taruni's face was turning red and her fingers were clutching the edge of the stair. Kunal could imagine why she would have got into such a fit – a recent incident might have triggered this reaction. "She is never happy with me and I mean it. She is always looking down at me with disdain, as if I was a mistake to begin with. It burns me on the inside. I want to go to her and for once, I want to, I want to –" squealed Taruni, gritting her teeth.

"Slap her?" Kunal finished her sentence. This fleeting notion in her mind sounded horrible when spoken out loud. Taruni felt disgusted that she could think about it, even if for a second. Her father had become a mere living puppet. He hardly spoke and was quiet most of the time. Frequent altercations between Taruni's mother and grandmother marred the atmosphere at home.

Her grandmother would vent to Taruni for hours at times. On the other hand, her mother would berate her for siding with her grandmother. No one could understand her agony at that point except Kunal.

"I will get away from here, just run away and never come back. I promise," said Taruni.

Our country has dream manufacturing industries, also known as colleges or universities. After high school, these industries lure potential employees by promising them a life of success. Hard-working students scramble for top grades to get a spot in reputed colleges. What about the millions of average-scoring students? They are left gawking at the stars, hoping for a good future for themselves. Fundamentally, no one's mental acumen should be judged by a few grades on a piece of paper, but that's not what happens. Would a ninety percenter be a better performer than a seventy percenter? Will he be more successful or be able to make better decisions? Who is to say that an average student could not surpass a top-grader with proper guidance? The answer to these questions is simple: numerous factors decide the outcome of one's choices. Can a person be judged on all these parameters based on a single test? Zilch. Nada. Zero.

The parents of an average student would employ all the resources, like money (sorry, donations!), political power, influence, contacts, etc., at hand to secure a lucrative position in a college. Students who cannot secure a position try their best year after year and then finally give up when nothing seems to work.

However, in the end, no matter what the outcome is, a person always finds their way. They have to – there's no choice. Life goes on. It does not pause or stop for any individual. One has to follow some path, any path, to achieve societal milestones and be satisfied with their lives. One has to be a winner, that's all. However, as humans, we fail each day but refuse to accept our shortcomings openly. Taruni thought that leaving her hometown for a decent college in a metro city would solve her problems. For her, it was a mission, a dream.

Now this is another topic altogether. For whom is one dreaming? Are they working towards their own dream or being compelled to follow someone else's? Blessed are those who have a straightforward answer to this. You need to chase your dreams, we hear. People much wiser than us continue to believe in this diktat and before they know it, their entire life washes past like a tsunami wave. Adults keep burdening their children to think about their futures while they are themselves still trying to understand life. In doing so, they deprive their offspring of choices and decisions and establish personal failure as a benchmark of judgement.

Yatin's aim was clear – he wanted to join the Indian Civil Service and get a government job.

Being the toughest examinations in the country, it was highly sought after and offered a prestigious career option for any individual.

In Yatin's life, that individual was his father. Since Yatin was ten, his father bore it in his skull to join the IAS. Yatin's father had a transport business and frequently conflicted with the police. He was sick of paying bribes and always wished to have direct contact with a high-ranking government official, like a city magistrate or a police commissioner. Who better to fill that role but his son? So long story short, Yatin's dream was to clear his board exams and then move to Delhi. He would enrol in any college for a namesake graduation degree while taking classes from a prestigious tuition centre. After completing his graduation, he would sit for the test and was confident of clearing it in one go.

"Ok, enough anger for one day… it's punch time," said Yatin. It was time to get over all the negativity. 'Punch' was the name of a signature drink offered by a juice vendor near their colony. It was a special mix of five different fruits. This strangely sweet, sour, and incredibly cold drink was an all-time stress buster for the trio. They raced to the destination on their bicycles, with Yatin arriving last. As they sat on a dilapidated metal bench, a child beggar came running and started asking for money. He was quite persistent in his coaxing ability.

"May God keep this couple happy," said the boy in a sing-song voice, frequently touching his lips to indicate hunger, and opening his palm requesting for some money.

"Who will keep me happy, this black shirt or blue shirt?" asked Taruni, pointing at Yatin and Kunal. "Stop messing around with the poor kid," scolded Kunal, while Taruni and Yatin laughed.

Kunal gave the boy a ten-rupee note and before they knew it, he returned with a couple more of his entourage, looking for alms. The shopkeeper had to chase all of them away before the other customers started complaining.

Taruni was watching the cars pass by. One day, she would own one of her own and drive it here to have 'punch' with her pals.

"Stop dilly dallying and finish your drink. Aunty's temperature will melt the thermometer if you are late," said Yatin, interrupting Taruni's daydream and handing over a finished assignment with her name on top.

Taruni had completely forgotten about the homework. Noticing her mood that day, Yatin had finished it for her while she was sharing her ordeal. He had even morphed his handwriting to match hers. Taruni smiled and kept the assignment in her bag. Despite all the annoying things in her life, she was blessed to have one great thing: her buddies.

But good things hardly last.

5

Khushi was Taruni's lab partner at school. She was one girl Taruni thoroughly enjoyed interacting with. They were both testing an algorithm in the computer lab. Lucky for Taruni, Khushi was expert in Python.

"So, what's new?" asked Khushi as she meticulously typed each line of the code onto a pale yellow keyboard.

"Just the usual. Struggling with chemistry. The after-school tuition is not working," replied Taruni.

"Chemistry is about –" started Khushi, pausing suddenly. Taruni looked at Khushi noticing the pause and realised she was caught peeking at Sahil.

"Well, well. Increased levels of dopamine and adrenaline might hinder a lot of other activities," said Khushi. They both laughed.

"It's nothing like that, but you know..." said Taruni.

"Listen, he is not into you. He doesn't even know you exist, let alone decipher your mysterious eye signals," replied Khushi.

Taruni felt attacked, but the observation was accurate. Whether it was the school assembly, fests, or free periods after class, she tried her best to interact with Sahil, but it was as if she was invisible to him. He would chat for a bit and then get back to his circle immediately, utterly oblivious to her hints of interest. Taruni knew he was still single, which is why his lack of interest was even more annoying.

"Why is that? Is something wrong with me?" continued Taruni.

"Well, you won't like it," replied Khushi.

"Go on, I'm a big girl," said Taruni, foreseeing a bitter truth coming her way. This was why she liked Khushi – direct and honest, unlike many other fellow students.

"Turn a little," said Khushi, typing side by side. Taruni followed her lead and spotted Kunal and Yatin heckling some other students, completely ignoring their assignment.

"What about them?"

"Look, don't stare – two handsome guys. Kunal is a broad-chested giant who hails from money, and Yatin is a fair, red-cheeked darling. Cherry on top – their sharp intellect. You are stuck to them all the time. Anybody observing you would know you don't have an iota of personal space left."

"But we are childhood friends. It is nothing..."

"I wish we were still children. But we are not. Mark my words, the day is not far when one of them will ask you out."

Taruni looked at her idiot friends. Yatin with his silky hair and broad smile; Kunal with his bulky shoulders and a sharp jawline – they looked like soldiers in training. Their transformation was not invisible, but it was never obvious to her. They both were her pals.

"I know it is difficult to handle. Having such close buddies is a gift. Let me share some gossip with you. These idiots have no clue how popular they are with the girls, but no one approaches them because –"

"Of me?" asked Taruni, shocked.

"No one understands your deal. It's common knowledge that a girl and a boy can never be 'just friends'," said Khushi.

Taruni had a retort on the tip of her tongue but refrained herself from speaking out loud. She did not want to spoil her friendship with Khushi by being glib, even though she clearly felt differently. She believed a boy and girl could remain friends for life. Any other notion was complete rubbish. Her bond of friendship was as pure as the Ganges, and probably stronger than what she had with her parents. No matter what she faced at home, she would break into a million pieces if the relationship with her buddies got messed up. Kunal and Yatin were her constants for life.

Friendship is one of the most exploited, misused, and underestimated of relationships. When a guy approaches his love interest, he usually begins with – can we be friends? When couples reach an impasse and confuse their feelings, their next question is – can we still be friends? We keep going down the wrong lane, weaving complex relationship architectures based on society's requirements when friendship, the central core of our existence, should be left untainted and pure. Human beings have a tendency to attach themselves to everything and everybody around them. All they need are connections of goodwill, gratitude, compassion, and love – that's it.

A good example of this is the bond we form with others as kids, bonds that sustain the test of time and continue to thrive as we grow up. We play, share, laugh, and spend hours with each other, cherishing every moment of our companionship. Friendship is not a stepping stone for love or a doormat to fall back to after a romantic relationship goes for a toss.

However, this revelation by Khushi struck a cord of fear in Taruni's heart. She wasn't fearful for herself, but for her pals. If she wasn't careful, this merciless society would soon claim another victim.

6

Yatin was studying in his room with only a single lamp as a source of light. To him, this lone bulb represented his father's watchful eye, constantly observing and reminding him of his unwavering dream. He tried to skim through a page of the newspaper, but the words shimmered, almost leaping out at him from darkened corners of the room. Several educational magazines were piled up on his left. To his right was a similar tower of study material from various coaching and tuition centres. His school books covered the front of his desk. He was living in a fort of academia. All he had was a little wriggle room to move his exhausted body and sometimes sleep with his eyes wide open.

Yatin had a happy and supportive family. Nothing mattered to him more than his dad's dream – he really wanted to make him proud. But the fear of failure haunted him. The success rate of clearing the UPSC exam is 0.01 percent. What if, despite all his hard work, he failed? While his peers would be pursuing engineering, architecture, and other professional degrees, he'd be spending time on a dummy graduation course, hoping to enter the civil services. If things didn't go as planned, he would have nothing to fall back to, no fancy college to enter, with a ruined life ahead of him.

'*Your dad is getting old.*' '*Soon everything will be on your shoulders.*' '*Start taking some responsibility.*' His mother's words echoed around him. The constant reminder of his inevitable destiny, now coupled with the looming doom of failure, was bending his back.

He was still gazing dumbstruck at the unread pile of study material beside his desk when his sister entered the room and added another magazine to his stash. According to his itinerary, he was supposed to mentally wolf down fifty magazines in a month. He had not even made a dent in this number. At most, he would go through the Bollywood section and then throw the magazine aside – not a good sign for someone dying to fulfil his dream.

The clock kept ticking and hours went by. It was time to meet Kunal and Taruni, but he decided to skip the rendezvous this time. He thumped a finished pile of magazines with his fist out of happiness – he had succeeded in completing his quota for the day. He moved to the computer table, switched on his computer, and logged into a racing game. Venting off some steam, he played for hours until his mother called him for dinner.

Yatin walked out of the basement and devoured his meal while his mother looked at him fondly. She was proud of her growing son and was happy to see his budding appetite – she thought of adding an extra chapati to his meals from next time. After dinner, Yatin went for a short walk, taking the back route to skip passing through Kunal's house. This route took him to the marketplace. The building had three floors, the topmost abuzz with much activity – a new joint had opened, which was frequented by numerous school goers. Its seclusion and location in the extreme corner of the building added to its allure. Tea, coffee, carbonated drinks, Maggi, and cigarettes were the top items on its menu card.

Yatin hesitated a bit before entering. He had found this place with his new friends from tuition. One of them challenged him to finish a cigarette, and he did. When the same friend dared him to stop, he couldn't. Yatin knew his father would skin him alive if he found out and his friends would disapprove, but the guilt vanished into thin air when a puff of polluted air entered his lungs. His aching brain got rid of its troubles for a while, which was a welcome relief. Or was it just his imagination?

"How was your day?" asked Akki in a languid tone, momentarily relaxed after a puff.

"It starts now. You tell me. Any luck with your girl?" asked Yatin.

"Nah, she blocked me on social media. I plan to create a fake account and stalk her," he replied, laughing. "I am not as lucky as other people. Look at that badass. Guess who he is talking to," challenged Akki.

Yatin shrugged, indicating he had no clue.

"Taruni."

"Impossible," said Yatin, taken aback. "He is faking it."

"You don't know him. He is a specialist. Not bestowed with the best of looks, but amazing at charming the pants off of people."

Yatin stood up suddenly, toppling the table as he did. He walked up to the boy and thumped him on the shoulder.

"What's up, my man?" said Yatin. The boy jumped at Yatin's impromptu approach.

"If you mess with Taruni, I'll shatter your world," said Yatin.

Onlookers peered at them with interest – they hadn't seen a brawl in ages. Two boys fighting over a girl made the best story.

"Chill, man. What does it have to do with you? Are you seeing each other?"

Yatin balled his hands into fists.

"No, right? She told me. Anyway, calm down. I need some time to assess if she's my type. There's nothing serious. You can chill," said the boy casually.

The instant his sentence ended, a massive blow struck him in the chest, knocking the daylights out of him. Everybody got thrilled and started hooting. Noticing the commotion, the manger entered and threw both of them outside the cafe.

"Don't set foot in this cafe again. I cannot allow anyone to hurt my customers," said the manager, folding his arms.

Yatin glanced at the sticker on a newly launched

pack of cigarettes and read the health advisory. Instead of heeding the warning, he noticed the irony between the owner's words and the product's advisory and left the building, laughing his guts out.

7

Yatin did not attend school the next day. He wanted to at least get up and play some video games, but his head had other plans – it was throbbing like crazy, as if his veins were aching to burst out of his brain. Medicine was barely effective. It appeared like the headache was there to stay for long. Every time he looked at his study table, his head would throb and he would be compelled to look away.

By four in the evening, Yatin was bored out of his wits, so he decided to go for a ride on his bicycle. He realised that the only solution to his lethargy was fresh air. On the way, at the corner of the road, there was a wooden stall. He stopped and asked for a cigarette. Noticing his age, the vendor charged him a bit extra. Yatin wanted to give him a piece of his mind, but he kept quiet and silently puffed on his contraband. Chewing some mint once he was done, he picked his bicycle and started towards his destination. When he reached the bridge, he noticed Taruni standing under it, glaring at him and just waiting to explode.

"What is it?" asked Yatin, gently kneading his temples.

Taruni shoved her phone close to his face. Yatin saw himself in a video. He pressed play and watched himself knock the stuffing out of the boy. He felt incredibly proud of himself.

"Oh, someone made a clip. What a smack," he said, punching the air with his fist and imitating his blow from yesterday.

"Idiot! Why did you hit him?" yelled Taruni.

"You are asking me? He was –"

"Talking to me. Yes. So?"

Yatin was taken aback for a bit. He was speechless. Why the hell was Taruni mad at him? He had done nothing wrong, he thought and composed himself.

"A random guy announces that my friend is talking to him. He then has the gall to say that he is gauging your type. I mean, wouldn't that piss me off? You should be glad that I stood up to him when he was being so derogatory towards you," said Yatin.

"Who are you to judge?" questioned Taruni.

"Just calm down, okay. I don't understand you at all. Why are you overreacting?"

"I am overreacting? Really? So what if he was checking me out? Did I ask for help? You need to understand, there are boundaries and…" she paused. Yatin was really shaken by her reaction.

"Is this the first time?" said Yatin softly, raising his head and interrupting Taruni. "I have been protecting you from bullies since we were kids. We used to find you crying alone on the steps on this very bridge. And you are explaining boundaries to me?" retorted Yatin. A tear glistened in his eyes.

"We grew up together, we know each other more than our parents do. And today, a guy who has known you for a week is coming between us? He is treating you like an object, but for him you are arguing with me!?" he continued.

"We grew up, Yatin! We are friends. That does

not mean you will make my decisions for me. That is the point. There is a boundary, a limit, a personal space. No one decides for me, but me," said Taruni.

"To hell with you and your space. I don't need to be a part of your sudden desperate hunt for boys. I will smack that guy again if need be. Don't ever come crying to me. Ooh, the world is unfair. Ooh, why is life like this? Ooh, no one understands me. Ooh, my mother traumatises me!" ridiculed Yatin.

Khushi's influence had moulded Taruni. She wanted to make new friends outside of Yatin and Kunal. How long could her social life be governed by just these two? All she wanted to do was casually converse with Sahil. There was no need for anyone to get hyper. Moreover, this decision was not wrong – she felt nice when she was speaking with other people. But no one could reason with Yatin's childish brain. Watching him mimic her insensitively sent her in a tizzy.

Bringing her mother into the picture – he had crossed all limits.

"I never want to see your face again!" said Taruni, quivering with anger.

"Likewise, sicko. Go have fun. Come Kunal, let's go," responded Yatin casually. Kunal, who had been observing this altercation silently, stared at the sunset.

"Are you coming or you want to take the side of Madam Boundaries?" said Yatin, taking a dig at Kunal too.

"Both of you are idiots. Just leave," said Kunal, eyeing Yatin. Taruni was still seething with anger and paced the floor.

"If Taruni wants to explore other relationships, she's not wrong. Plus she didn't lie about it. She didn't hide like you or be ashamed of it. Don't you think I know what you were doing in that shop? The pressure of civil services and your family's expectations is killing you. Accept it. Instead of doing the right thing, you are trying to hide your filthy habit from your friends. This is as good as betrayal, right?" blasted Kunal. He then turned to Taruni.

"And you. You are no less. First you stop believing in your mother and your hometown, and now Yatin? Yes, it is okay to explore and experiment, but you should never forget your roots or where you've come from. Don't think that the grass is always greener on the other side because it may not be. The relationships we build should be cultivated and not chucked at the drop of a hat. Making new relationships should not be at the expense of the existing ones. That does not solve problems but only creates more. All this talk about personal space and boundaries is a testament to us growing up. But it shouldn't be realised at the cost of our loved ones. You never let go of your friends and family, the time you've spent with them, and the memories you've made. In the end, this is the only thing that matters," he completed.

The sun finally set at the end of Kunal's tirade. It was almost like it was sick of the argument and didn't wish to witness any more of it. Taruni and Yatin were humbled by Kunal's words. They had nothing more to say. Yatin slowly walked towards his bike and picked it up. As he rode back home, he stopped near the stall again. The vendor welcomed him with a smile. Yatin parked his bicycle and went to the backside of the stall. He had tears in his eyes and a storm of smoke in his lungs. His inability to control both made him hate himself. The worst part of life is when your loved ones act like strangers.

Taruni stepped down from the bridge and walked towards her dad's office. As the breeze hit her back, she felt better. She wanted to turn and feel it on her face, but she had already chosen her path.

8

What is right or wrong, good or bad? Even though we have a well-established code of conduct, nothing can be accurately defined. Intentions and circumstances don't always work in each other's favour and could sometimes become the reason behind one's downfall. Yet we love to classify and judge everything to befit our human nature. Honesty is the best policy they say, but do we agree? Are we always truthful? We talk about peace while manufacturing tools of violence, glorifying in every sphere of life, be it in cinemas or in real life. Treating everyone equally is often talked about, yet we discriminate on the basis of gender, class, colour, etc.

These divisions and classifications consume our very existence and anchor our dreams. It's not easy to comprehend why we have them in our lives. Look at humans, each demographic has a set target and amount of expectations, which they try to achieve based on their potential, location, and social status. If a person born in a family of limited means can make something of themselves without formal education, it's applauded and considered worthy of appreciation. However, a child born to a high-class family will have different life goals, which are probably governed by a set of rules pre-defined by the society they live in. Those who break these rules become rebels and are looked up to. That's the irony of our society. It forces you to heed its decree but then languishes respect when you go against it by breaking the rules.

A student hailing from a family of medical practitioners would not receive the same respect for topping a university as compared to one born in a family of cobblers. Such stories reflect the failures and limitations of society. They encourage people to follow their dreams but quickly douse their fire by stating the underhanded truth – life is unfair.

Two points to be noted – one, no success story can be replicated; two, the instant one reveals their deepest desires, people try their level best to take advantage of it. Many motivational speakers, life coaches have identified this basic human flaw as one of the best opportunities to earn money and build a reputation.

To state an example, when a motivational speaker raised his hand after narrating the powerful story of Steve Jobs and Elon Musk – their lives, the betrayal, and how they conquered the market – the students were quaking with hope and excitement.

He had come to their school as part of an event organised by the teachers.

"You can do this too. The possibilities are endless, the futures are many. But do you have it in your HEART to see it through?" he asked, and the students jumped off their seats. The teachers who had organised the event glanced at the principal, convinced that much appreciation and a good increment was sure to come their way. Yes, they had spent quite a fortune on this speaker and it appeared that he had come through.

"You have one life! Let me tell you, do not let it go. A young heart rarely brakes, so charge ahead will full throttle. Work, play, go to the gym, get a hobby, go trekking, explore places, meet new people, choose a path, set a goal, and just go for it – every single day and every single night – there's magic at the end of the tunnel," he narrated, circling his fist in the air as if creating a tsunami.

Kunal was infuriated on hearing this nonsense. A decade ago, there were hardly any such speakers. People were motivated and dedicated to their vocation like Steve and Elon of their own accord. They didn't need anybody to show them the way. These fancy words, dialogues, how relevant are they in real life? This speaker himself – how much life had he seen himself? Were his experiences more valuable than those who thought they had failed in life? Kunal preferred to get the guidance of an unsuccessful adult than this showman. He looked at his peers. These fools whose aspirations were dancing naked in their eyes. They had no clue what it meant to struggle to achieve their goals.

"What if your parents don't allow you to pursue your dream?" yelled Kunal during a break in the speech. He didn't need a microphone, the scepticism in his voice was loud enough. A teacher would have reprimanded him under ordinary circumstances, but this was a public event.

"There is a time for Q&A," interrupted the moderator, silently hiding her anger.

"No, no, it is okay. Absolutely fine. That is an honest question. I am happy that my words have shaken something inside him," said the speaker and turned towards Kunal.

"Friend, you need to persevere. Be patient and make them listen. In the end, they will see what it is that you really want. People will always try to stop you, especially parents, because they can't see the bigger picture. They may not understand your choice today, but if you tread carefully in the right direction, you'll be able to make them see the reason. Does this answer your question?".

"No, it doesn't," said Kunal, smacking the applause away. The speaker pressed his lips and gave a strained smile.

"Let me repeat. People around you, including your

loved ones, might not see your vision, but if your dream is strong, you will find your way. Because the only right way is to keep walking forward."

"I am really sorry sir, but have you ever faced a calamity in life? The amount of pressure a student handles daily, he literally gets smothered by the burden of expectations. The list you mentioned for living a good life – no one cares. Our goals, dreams – again, no one cares. I need 99% marks to get admission in the college of my choice, and this is a fact. You said we shouldn't worry, and that a college dropout can also make a fortune. Such individuals are at most 1% of the total dropouts. What about the rest of them? Again, let us not be concerned about the facts. Loved ones do not care about our dreams if they do not align with their mindsets," said Kunal, turning towards the audience with anger.

"Take a step, he says and you are all clapping. Can you tell me what step you are planning to take?

If one is not allowed to attend tuitions because the family has signed off on his life to manage the business, what is he supposed to do? Should I beg for tuition money after school and start lying to achieve my goal of becoming a scientist? Will someone shower money on me in my sleep?"

In his haste, Kunal had given away the subject of his narrative – the word 'I' revealed his truth in front of everyone, even to those who were unaware of his family situation. Taruni and Yatin realised that Kunal was on the verge of tears. Despite what they were going through, Taruni could not watch him in pain and lowered her gaze. For the first time, she had witnessed and was swept away by Kunal's ability to swallow his anguish and still speak out publicly. It was as if a layer had vanished and various shackles had emerged underneath, coiling on the floor and getting attached to everyone's limbs. We were bound by them, no matter how free we felt.

Yatin had been enjoying the speaker's stories but had come to his senses after listening to Kunal's outburst. Whether Kunal was right or wrong, it didn't matter. What mattered was the truth behind his words and what the burden of expectations could do to a sane person.

Everybody in school could empathise with Kunal's plight. The speaker became nervous and didn't know how to respond. Though he had enough experience to change the course of the discussion, it was not needed. Kunal handed the microphone to a fellow student and rushed out of the auditorium.

9

One can always take a minute of their time to call someone and enquire about their health and let them know how they feel – anything else is just an excuse. After she left home, Taruni got used to the lifestyle she considered annoying before. She woke up in the morning, washed her clothes, cooked food, cleaned the dishes, walked long distances to save money, always reciprocated with a smile, and even started acting differently in public as opposed to in private. All this sacrifice for the one thing she longed for the most – her freedom.

Now, back in her hometown, she had nothing to do. Their family had a maid – a young girl of about Taruni's age – who practically did all the household chores. She was also her mother's 'bff' who would discuss the daily soaps with her. It appeared that the maid was closer to her mother than Taruni and maybe it was true. Evidently, her mother was still adjusting to the shock of having Taruni at home.

Two days had passed and her father was still unconscious. The doctor said he would gain consciousness the next day, but it was time for Taruni to leave. She could not ignore her classes any more. Her flatmates were always arguing about going back home and would be homesick most of the time but the feeling was different for Taruni. She had always wanted to run away from her hometown. Whether a good decision or bad, she knew this change was the best thing that had happened to her. Still, a question loomed in her mind. Why had she come back so easily? What was the trigger that had made her pack her bags in a heartbeat and take the next train home? Especially a place that had driven her up the wall and had no special place in her life anymore. It appeared her efforts had been in vain because her dad refused to open his eyes and her mother clearly did not need any emotional support.

Some say that life is about meeting new people and gaining new experiences. For Taruni it was the opposite – she had lost the closest people in her life. After the fight with Yatin, she had walked away and never looked back at the bridge. She made new friends and joined other groups. The entire school noticed their separation. She even avoided meeting Kunal and Yatin before leaving to Delhi. Sometimes it's imperative to separate from the bondages in life in order to explore uncharted waters. Attachments are only impediments in the path to growth, or so she thought.

That day when she walked away – what if she had turned back? What if she had handled Yatin's hot-headedness differently? Her interaction with Sahil ended in a week. There was nothing serious there. She would be reminded of her close friends everywhere she went – something or the other would trigger their memories in her mind. She was unable to get them out of her system. But did she want them back in her life?

No. She kept reasoning with her subconscious, failing to understand the root cause of the quarrel. She decided to go for a walk to blow off some steam and unintentionally trudged along a familiar path from the days gone by. Nostalgia hit her like a brick and flooded her mind with countless memories. She felt a rush of adrenaline and couldn't understand why her heart was still being pulled by this place.

Before she knew it, she had reached the wall that separated her society from the railway station. Looking through a gap her eyes fell on something unexpected. Yatin was standing on the bridge, looking at her. His skin glowed under the sun.

Looking at him, she could only feel one emotion – regret. Why did she have to come back to this town and to this bridge?

There were enough reasons to turn back, but she continued to walk up to the bridge. The warmth of the early morning sun was slowly dissolving the chill of last night creating an enigmatic atmosphere. Aroma of far-off places emanated from the train tracks. Taruni sighed with relief despite Yatin's blazing, red face.

"How have you been?" asked Taruni, greeting her friend out of courtesy.

"Why are you here?" responded Yatin. He

displayed no sign of happiness, unlike Kunal at the station.

"I can ask you the same," she replied, smiling wryly. They remained silent and looked away. Taruni realised that Yatin's animosity had not ebbed a bit. What was she supposed to do if he refused to grow up? It was possible that he hated her more than she hated him. This reaction was not unusual to her. On the bright side, Kunal was walking towards them.

"What a coincidence," said Kunal. Gauging their body language, he laughed. "Fine, not a planned one, but it looks like a reunion."

"Reunion is for old friends. Not for those who betray each other for petty things," said Yatin, irritatingly. This hurt Taruni a little, but she maintained her composure. It had been months since someone had been this upfront with her.

"Look at her, man. She is one stone-hearted person," mocked Yatin. "Smiling as if she has achieved something great."

"Bummer I'm not a heroine from one of the movies you watch. Don't know how you would have reacted to her when you can't even stand the sight of a simple girl who was once your friend," replied Taruni, looking away.

"Yeah, I bet," retorted Yatin, clasping the railing of the bridge.

"Just let it go both of you!" shouted Kunal out of frustration.

"Well, I was only supposed to meet you, Kunal but now that she's also here, I'd better give someone a piece of my mind before they decide to escape again. This woman ruined the best part of my life – school. Whenever I think about it, I am filled with rage and a sense of betrayal. Our best friend did not give a damn about our feelings and left us both alone. I don't know how you are okay with this. She avoided us in school for more than a year, roamed around with people who would bitch about her behind her back, people who I fought with for her, and didn't even meet us before she left town. Guess what? I commit to my relationships, and I do not forgive betrayal," said Yatin.

Taruni watched Yatin berating her from the bottom of his heart. She knew that truth was bitter, but had never expected it to be this acrid. It was scary and heart wrenching. She had two options – be honest, walk away and leave this world as she had found it, or stand her ground and face this impediment head-on whether she liked it or not.

The tiny realisation of regret might have further implications, but there was nothing she could not tackle later. She decided to stay and give Yatin what he wanted – even if it was fake and dishonest. With slow steps, Taruni walked towards Yatin and hugged him. He was taken aback and subconsciously lifted his hands in the air, trying not to touch her. She tightened her grip and Yatin's muscular body froze under the pressure of the sudden embrace.

"When we are children, things are different. Later, when we grow up, life teaches us a lot of lessons that enrich our journey. Tell me Yatin, you've also done things that were considered wrong but never confessed. Why? Because you didn't want to. If you restrain yourself for the sake of people, that is cheating. We are told our goal is achieved after finishing school, then after college, then after marriage, then after kids, and then we just wait to die. The world does nothing but slowly manipulates us towards our death," said Taruni.

"Boy, that is heavy," remarked Kushal. Taruni turned on her heels and looked at Kunal.

"We all are changing; I just have the guts to accept it. I do not feel guilty about doing so because there is nothing wrong with it. Look at you, the one who took the biggest hit but is hiding it all behind a smile. Do you think we don't know how you must have felt giving up your dream and joining your dad's business?" asked Taruni.

Kunal shrugged, looking away.

There was too much to resolve, too many shackles to break. So many scenarios, perspectives, and feelings, very few words to express them, and even less time. Perfect stories have a structure, character development graph, high stakes, and a proper ending – life is never like that. We just lie to ourselves trying to look for nirvana only to make our lives worse and more complicated.

A train came into the station, slowed down, and then stopped completely. Some people deboarded and then it left. Taruni's vision was clear – Kunal was sitting on the stairs and Yatin was looking at her. There was peace, if only for a moment.

Change Stories – Next Reads

Kuroopa

'Why did God make me so ugly? Am I not your daughter? Was I exchanged at the hospital? Or did you leave me in the sun one day and that's why I became so dark?'

Meera, one of three siblings, has been struggling with her identity since childhood. She is subjected to mean, insensitive remarks by neighbours, relatives, and random people around her due to the lack of pleasing physical attributes. Constant comparison with her fair, blue-eyed sister further deteriorates her relationship with friends, family, and most importantly, herself.

A shocking incident involving the household pets pushes Meera over the edge, forcing her parents, especially her father, to take action and bring her back to reality.

Will Meera be able to find her footing in this hypocritical world that preaches "looks don't matter" while constantly objectifying and running towards beautification? Will she be able to accept herself for who she is and overcome the hatred she has for herself?

A Gutterful Life

Hindus and Muslims live in harmony across an open gutter (naala) at the edge of the city.

Whether it's the story of Somu and Aklaq – two innocent souls from different religions who stumble into each other on the naala and foster a friendship like no other; Billu and Arif – two budding businessmen trying to make a living – who are subjected to inter-community politics through the tryst of fate; or the community's favourite Chai-Chachu – an old tea-seller with unknown origin but an important story to tell, *A Gutterful Life* brings forth a plethora of sentiments culminating in an emotional climax.

Will Aklaq and Somu's friendship survive the vagaries of communal division? Will Chai-Chachu be able to bridge the gap between Hindus and Muslims across the naala? Will religious propaganda compel people to forget their hardships and sow seeds of division in the illusion of unity?

First Love Many Times

'She is my life; she is my love. What will I do if I fail? True love only happens once in a lifetime.'

Abhi falls head-over-heels in love with Kavya at first sight. They become friends and everything is beautiful as if they were destined to be together. Until the day Abhi confesses his love for her at the Taj Mahal.

Catastrophe befalls and Abhi's dream shatters. Completely heartbroken, Abhi decides to fight for his love one last time, like the ones shown in movies. If successful, life would be beautiful again, else he would have to end his life.

Will Abhi be able to understand the difference between true love and the one displayed on screen? Will he see reason beyond his anguish? Does love truly happen just once?

This short story debates the question about first love and the trials and tribulations one goes through to achieve it.

A Mother By The Window

'A final lesson for her, she thought. A woman's happiness resides outside herself, in places defined by society.'

Neetu, an obedient housewife, devotes all her time and energy to take care of her family. She is diligent and abides by the rules society has laid out for her. Nostalgia of winning a beauty pageant many years ago and regret of marrying early encourages her to try her hand at becoming an influencer on Instagram.

She works hard to achieve her new goal, without disrupting the life she was married into. Her attention eventually gets divided between her dream and family, bringing to light the secret she is harbouring. The secret hurts her image of an "ideal wife" much to her husband's chagrin.

With Neetu's life in turmoil, Rahul takes a stand to save his mother's dream.

Will Neetu realise her true potential and achieve her dream? Are women expected to fulfil only one role at a time, and no other? Does a woman's personal life belong only to her family? Is there any hope for change?

Also by

Kapil Raj

Now, a national bestseller.

Life was a fun fed roller coaster: new found love, drugs, cat-fights, patch ups, crushes, night hangouts, and unplanned trips. Like any girl, not in the wildest dream, palak could imagine that after attending a rave party, she will wake up to the horror of finding herself raped.

In traumatic conditions and struggle between sanity and hallucinations, she is compelled by the circumstances to leave her world. Already fighting a war within, her stances take a toll witnessing horrifying tales of women and girls. Little did she know that this catastrophe was not enough for one lifetime, and a storm — was just cooling its heels.

Will she be able to carve her path while facing the rapists, her tyrant father, appearances of her passed away mother? Should palak let her life to be decided by people, society, and taboos? Would justice return her life or revenge lend her peace?

A heart-rending story of a girl, whose beliefs and honor has been battered, stands up to make choices, rediscovering the meaning of life.

About the Author

Kapil Raj is a professional, speaker and writer-activist based in Delhi-NCR, India. With the heart of a philosopher, mind of a realist, and a deep-rooted non-conformist, he lives many lives, yet stealing the time for the most precious thing that matters to him: crafting plots, playing with characters, and weaving the stories based on intricate social subjects and challenging the dogmas.

His debut novel *ENDURER A Rape Story* is critically acclaimed by the media and loved by the readers. He is a noted speaker and delivered lectures in prestigious institutions and colleges.

Connect with him on Facebook, Twitter, Instagram @ikapilraj